Work Your Body, Grow Your Brain

Written by Erin Boodey
Illustrated by John Konecny

Published by Orange Hat Publishing 2012

ISBN 978-1-937165-23-9

Printed in the United States of America

www.orangehatpublishing.com

Dear Parents,

Play provides the foundation for learning and is an important aspect for childhood development. Exercise during play provides a positive influence on children's physical development; this leads the way to future healthy choices and habits. This book intends to give you a variety of ideas for playful interactions with your child while working to strengthen their motor skills. The development of fine motor, gross motor, and visual motor skills not only impacts your child's physical performance, but will improve classroom performance too. Remember to keep the atmosphere positive and have fun!

If you have concerns regarding your child's ability and/or performance with the activities, talk with your child's physician; an occupational therapy or physical therapy evaluation may be beneficial.

Prioritize safety! Age and ability level must be carefully considered prior to engaging in any of the suggested activities. Please consult with your child's physician if you have any doubts or questions.

Erin Boodey,
Author and Occupational Therapist

I like to work my body and move!
Moving makes my muscles and brain
grow big and strong.

I work my arms and shoulders.

I can walk like a bear. Can you try too?

I can walk on my hands.
My friend holds my knees
or ankles.

This is called a wheelbarrow walk.
How far can you go?

I can walk like a crab.
Can you go forward and
backward?

I work my eyes. I can see the shadow that matches the picture. Do you?

I can see 6 differences between these two pictures.
Can you find what is different?

I can find the squirrel and the shovel.

Can you find the:
Dog
Bird
Frog
Kite
Banana

Can you count how many:
Boys
Girls
Bubbles

I work my hands
and fingers.

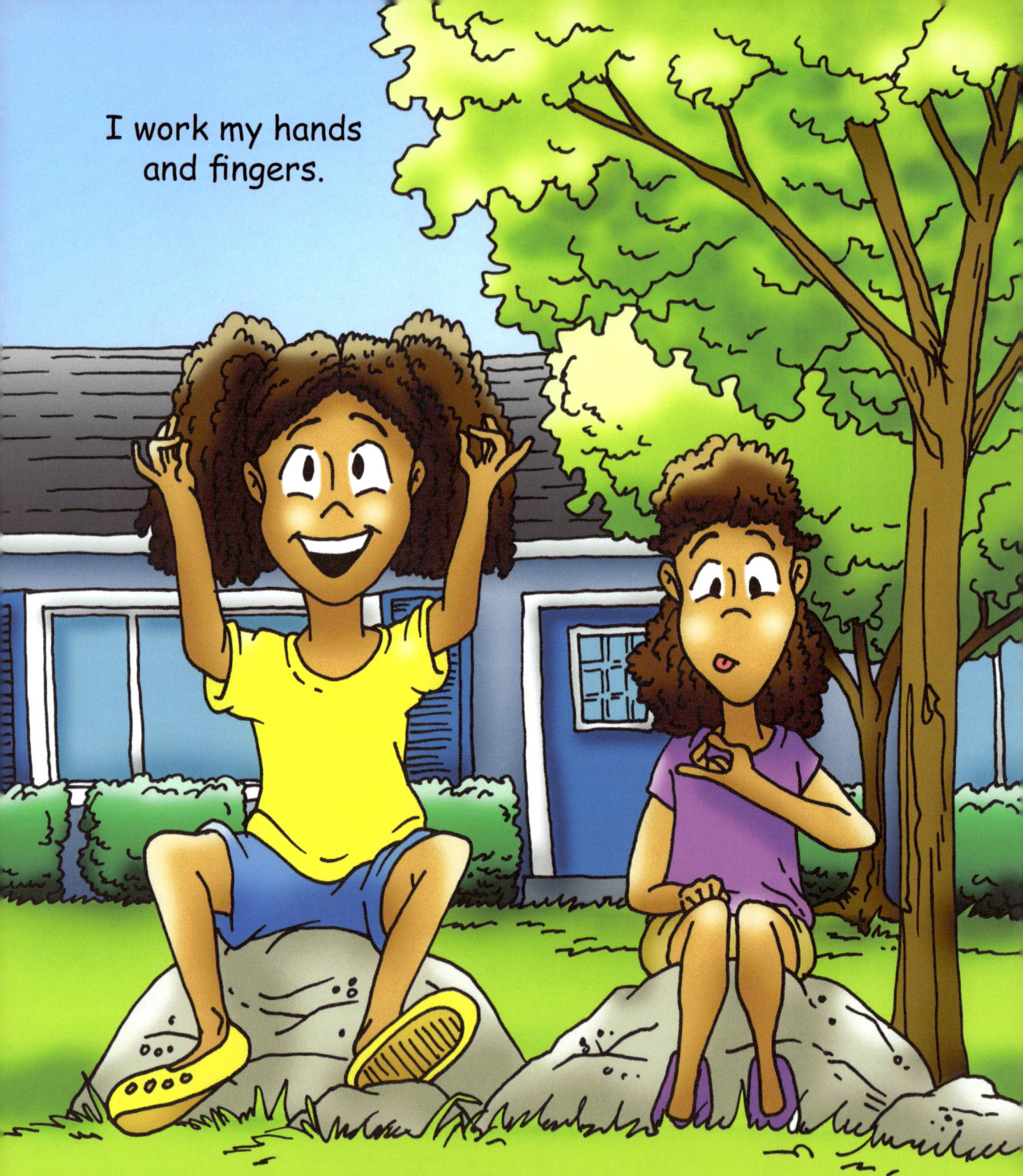

I can touch each finger to my thumb.
Can you try both hands at the same time?

I can pick up many coins with only one hand.
I put them into my piggy bank.
How many can you pick up in one hand?

I can color pictures and draw.

I use a tiny crayon for my small hand.

I can put cereal onto a string to make a necklace. But sometimes I eat it!

I can play "Simon Says . . . " Listen carefully.

I work my legs.

I can kick a ball. It's your turn.

I can hop like a frog.

Ribbit!

I work my whole body.

I can ride my bike.

I can make an obstacle course.

Go under.

Go over.

Jump!

I work my mouth and lips.
I can blow objects off the table with a straw.
Can you try it with a paper ball or tissue?

I can try new food even if I don't think I will like it.

FOODS I'VE TRIED...

★ CARROTS	FISH
CELERY	★ CHICKEN
★ YAMS	PORK
	BROCCOLI
★ PEAS	★ ASPARAGUS
TOMATO	
AVACADO	★ POTATO

Sometimes it turns out to be my favorite food!

Your brain is connected to your body. When you move your body you work your brain!

Using our whole body makes us strong and healthy boys and girls.

www.ingramcontent.com/pod-product-compliance
Lightning Source LLC
Chambersburg PA
CBHW042000100426
42813CB00019B/2938